How the Dead Bury the Dead

Akron Series in Poetry

How the Dead Bury the Dead

WILLIAM GREENWAY

The University of Akron Press
Akron, Ohio

ACKNOWLEDGMENTS

Aethlon: "Tough"; *Ambergris:* "Between Pittsburgh and Cleveland"; *American Poetry Review:* "How the Dead Bury the Dead"; *The Bridge:* "Father Dreams iii"; *Calapooya Collage:* "Athletes Dying Young"; *California State Poetry Quarterly:* "The Magic Flute"; *The Cape Rock:* "Father Dreams vi, vii, viii"; *Embers:* "Father Dreams i, v, ix"; *Father Dreams* (State Street Press, 1994): "Father Dreams i–ix," "Yards," "Anniversaries," "Tying a Tie," "Hardheads," "Athletes Dying Young"; *Fine Madness:* "Driving Toward the Ocean in the Afternoon," "Winter in the South," "The Goodwin Sands," "Dying in the Fish Restaurant"; *Florida Review:* "Nineveh"; *Fresh Ground:* "Epistle to the Church at Smyrna (Georgia)"; *The Journal:* "Heart Shot"; *Kansas Quarterly:* "Prayers"; *Laurel Review:* "All of Us Are Children," "The Original Adam and Eve," "The Texas Chainsaw Revival"; *Licking River Review:* "Father Dreams iv"; *Mahoning Valley Poetry* (The Bacchae Press, 1993): "Anniversaries," "Yards"; *New Myths/MSS:* "Every Reason"; *New Virginia Review:* "Tying A Tie"; *Oxford Magazine:* "Advent"; *Piedmont Literary Review:* "Tool"; *Pig Iron:* "Rust Belt"; *Pikeville Review:* "Father Dreams ii"; *Poet & Critic:* "Hands"; *Poetry:* "Small Road to Nowhere," "Intensive Care," "Entrance," "Hypochondria," "Anniversary 2," "Seventh Heaven," "One Owner," "For My Friends, Who Complain That I Never Write Anything Happy"; *Poetry Northwest:* "Hardheads," "Tenderhooks"; *Poets On:* "Archeology"; *Prairie Schooner:* "Yards"; *Rain In Most Places* (March Street Press, 1992): "Disserth," "The Goodwin Sands"; *Slant:* "First Love"; *South Florida Poetry Review:* "The Place Names of Dreams"; *Southern Humanities Review:* "Anniversary 1"; *Southern Poetry Review:* "Apnea," "Bayou"; *Southern Review:* "Disserth"; *Spoon River Poetry Review:* "Fortified Hills," "Child of Many Prayers," "Elementary"; *Xavier Review:* "Skin," "New House on the Market"; *Youngstown Poetry* (The Bacchae Press, 1992): "Rust Belt."

All inquiries and permissions requests should be addressed to the Publisher, The University of Akron Press, 374B Bierce Library, Akron, Ohio 44325-1703.

LIBRARY OF CONGRESS CATALOGING IN PUBLICATION DATA
Greenway, William. 1947–
How the dead bury the dead / William Greenway. — 1st ed.
p. cm. — (Akron series in poetry)
ISBN 1-884836-01-1 (cloth: alk. paper): $19.95. — ISBN 1-884836-02-X (paper: alk. paper): $10.95
I. Title. II. Series.
PS3557.R3969H69 1994
811'.54—dc20 94-27058
CIP

Manufactured in the United States of America

FIRST EDITION

For Betty (again)

Contents

I *Father Dreams*

But one thing I pray for especially: since they say it is here
That the King of the Underworld's gateway is to be found,
Among these shadowy marshes where Acheron comes flooding through,
I pray for one look, one face-to-face meeting with my dear father.
Teach me the way and open the holy doors wide.

Aeneid, Book VI, lines 107–11 (translation by Seamus Heaney)

I throw myself on your breast my father,
I cling to you so that you cannot unloose me,
I hold you so firm till you answer me something.

Leaves of Grass, Walt Whitman

. . . whatever
returns from oblivion returns
to find a voice:

"The Wild Iris," Louise Glück

Yards

He had no luck with yards.
I made sure my first
was flat, square, spongy, etched
with mower tracks, daffs
already sprouting. But the last owner
took his thumbs with him, and I fear
the curse, the lawn already
tilting into a hill that sluices
rain, turns Georgia-red, gullies,
bleeds. My father's bulbs popped up
and rolled away like turnips
through fire ant cones, over
fireweed and gristle of crabgrass runners.
No matter what he threw down, fescue,
St. Augustine, Kentucky Bluegrass,
we'd come home to find it draining
seeds and manure into the neighbor's
turf thick as peat. Why weren't
we happier? The mower slid sideways
down the hill, bogged its tricycle
tires, the blade spit rock
into his shins, spewed dust in his face.
I went back to one, the worst,
catty-cornered on the lot, and stared
at the perfect lawn, the hill he swore at, called
impossible, now flat as a green.
Even his grave is bare.

Child of Many Prayers

When we got to where we could talk
of how different we are, she'd tell again,
as if to prove I was really hers,
how she stood on her head to get
me, the night she spent on the couch
where they'd made love, her legs up to help
the seed upstream, how when I brought home
pictures from the first grade, she sat down
on the same couch and cried for half
an hour at how beautiful I was, how
much I'd grown already. She stooped and
gathered my hair from the barber's floor,
and even when she whipped me she'd be
thinking—I have a son, like Hannah who was
barren till she promised God the strange
child who'd grow to hear voices in the dark.

Now, she can barely remember me,
a smudge in the family photo, one of those
blank faces in *Invasion of the Body Snatchers,*
except, for her, my features aren't
developing, rising through spinal fluid
clear as vinegar, but sinking, slippery
into dark water, melting like the faces of those
movie aliens bubbling back into the pod.
I'm seven already, and she's watching
while I stand in the pool, being
ducked in the warm Jordan painted
on the walls to seem flowing away past
palms, diminishing into the distance
that might be mountains, or could be clouds.

Elementary

Monday they'd bring a quarter—I'd carry
another bag, creased and wet
from my fist, or box that was a tin
cartoon of leftovers. Down a long
row I walked for milk, past steel
pans steaming real food. Anything
gets old, perfect meatloaf, vine ripe
tomatoes—under desks they
harden, soften, exchange chemicals.
Some days I'd dump it all, even sandwiches
my blond mother made in darkness,
unopened into drums of pig slop and beg
hard rolls like Luke Butler,
who stank, had green clothes, free hot
lunches, and blackheads, volcanoes pricked
with pepper. I still get sick of what
I make myself, and crave, not Antoine's
or Maxim's, but the dawn bacon of summer
camps, mess halls, the cafeterias of prisons,
mental institutions, homes for the old.
And what is heaven but another leftover?
Although I hope it's a sort of higher school,
one you walk to with both hands open.

Midway

Why do I react so violently
when asked to go?
I say that it's boring,
all those rides and stalls and sausage booths,
but I don't act bored, I act mad,
still mad at the man who ran the bumper cars,
with his whiskey breath, tattooed hands
rough on my legs, getting lost, diarrhea
from the corn dogs and cotton candy,
no toilet anywhere, loud screams
from the haunted house, breaking glass,
the aisles of penned livestock,
nothing fair about it.
But most of all my parents,
not fighting now but lurching, arms
around themselves, laughing at the squirmy
canvas paintings of the freaks,
her short shorts, their faces above me
orange and blue in the midway lights,
having their ages guessed,
my mother sad because they got it right,
my father not shooting rifles or basketballs
because he knew the bears would always be
for someone else. Wooden bottles,
rubber frogs, a stage of women with the eyes
of peacock fans. But most for how
they loved it anyway, and me ashamed,
looking up, looking on. It's not the fair
so much as them I don't want to see,
tacky-loving, younger than me.

Anniversaries

1.
It's hard to believe you've missed my wife
and your grandson, twenty-five years of fishing
and funny movies.
Every day you sleep
past breakfast, past supper.
What are you listening to
down in your room, your head
tilted toward the dark?
What dream is so beautiful it cannot spare you?

2.
Soon I'll be the age you are
forever, the day you pulled
off the interstate, your heart
boiling like a cracked block,
to die in a phone booth
while everyone passed you by.

We'll be twins—
I see us coming in the amber of store windows.
The next day I'll be
the eldest, you
tagging along to some
place you've already been.

Already you could be my mother's son.
Someday you could be mine.
Maybe then you'd listen
when I told you to stay
off the fatty foods and the interstates,
to slow down and stay well.
To grow old. To call.

Father Dreams

i

I still dream about his
failure. We are so poor
we must live in the park.
Someone has betrayed him
again. It's always cloudy,
the trees bare, their leaves
rusted shavings over the grass.
Each night we sleep on tombs
stained lime with mold, pull up
the quilts my mother weaves
from the spidery stuffing
of Spanish moss. I keep
saying to him it's
O.K., we're still alive. We're
all alive: it's so clear to me.
Yet he goes on, and we lie on tombs
under moss, listening as he wanders
all night, his voice
dwindling among the trees
as he drinks and weeps
the way he never would.

Father Dreams

ii

Adieu, adieu, adieu! remember me.
—Hamlet

You're taking me on a tour, the
landscape of your life, joking
about the greatest scenes:
the place you got caught
in a storm, *Here's where*
the wind blows when it rains.
Of the willow pond where you
fished, *Here's where the ducks*
have feet, though you can't
see them. At the house where
you were born you say,
There. That's where ghosts
swing from a clothesline all night.

Father Dreams

iii

I go to a high school gym
and you're already there watching
somebody play Wake Forest.

I think I'm sitting with you
but when I look around you're
a few rows up and back and don't seem
to see me. I should have been
a better player.

I move to try to get closer.
Wake Forest has one player over
seven feet with a huge
pot. I say loud enough for you
to hear, this guy's so old he's
grizzled, and everyone laughs
but you.

He wears a sheet, no one knows
why, bermuda shorts, and flip-flops
slapping the boards as he runs
up and down. They're so far
behind it's funny, can't buy
a basket.

This guy really needs
a beer, I say louder, looking
to see if you've heard
but you're gone,
just at the best part,
where the guys in sheets come back and win.

Father Dreams

iv

I was watching television late
into the night the way he did,
when he came and sat down again
in his big chair and we both watched,
afraid to look at him or speak
that he'd disappear, till he said,
This is Our Town. *It's better*
than I remember. Then a groan,
I'm so tired. I asked, *Doing what?*
But he just said it was all
right, that he had a helper, a
sidekick, like a cowboy. His thick
boots were greasy and dusty as old
tires, denim clothes blurry
with wear, ministering hands
now black. The weariness in his face
so bad it was decay. I begged him
to stay, rest, but he said he had
to go, that dawn was coming,
that to go back
was a long walk.

Father Dreams

v

My mother is a fish.
—As I Lay Dying

My father is a skeleton.
Traveling all his life he
died on the road, lies not
here, near me, but in a box
in the Georgia foothills, except
on the nights he comes in his old
flesh, with maps, pointing to
the capillaries of distance
he says we can cover in one
night. So we go.
In the old Mercury I fiddle
with his tapes and books on how
to grow rich on the slick front
seat while he drives, telling me
about deals, lost in the rain.
Soon the cocoa rivers rise, washing out
all bridges, signs. I look over
to where he was, turn the car around
to try to find my way home
or to Florida on my own
or by another way.

Father Dreams

vi

Sitting in a wheelchair
in a grove of winter trees,
a white-haired man watched
all of us passing.
In the next town
they told me it was you,
changed, that you hadn't died
on the road, but didn't
want to burden me.
By the time I got back
you were buried.

So I missed your second
life, but not your second
death. A life you said
is like a good car—
it never comes back.
And death?
Like trucks on the highway
there's always another.

Father Dreams

vii

I can finally talk after all
these years—like long
distance, there's always
a wait. Quickly,
it's different here, even
the tornadoes, purple
as eggplant, pearly as conch
shells you can slide through.
But I can only tell
three things and that was one.
My failure has nothing to do
with you. And April 15,
by the log jetty at the lake.
Try a top-water minnow in the shallows
just before dark.

viii

I think I've figured out
why I keep dreaming you're alive,
why we're always surprised when you
speak from your chair in the
dark corner. It's because of that last
year, sleeping in the den all day
because your nights were so bad,
the burning in your chest,
through with food and living
on chalk and milk like babies.
The last time I saw you
the tree lights tinted the white
hair of your sleeping head,
the laughter swirled around
you, white as a sheet, or
the ghost of Christmas past,
or future.

Father Dreams

ix

I was fifteen again, climbed out
my window, went riding my bike
through the whole night, first the black
bones of the city, rusted construction
skeletons, dinosaur machines black as tar,
then through streets with shadows
of gangs, out into the country, sand roads
pearl in the moon, through fences from
field to field past sleeping cows,
bogging down my tires till I was lost, my bike
broken. I was crying for you, my arm around
the fuzzed and muscled neck of a cow whose big
eye cried with me when Robert came
by in our '50 Chevy with the shift
on the column, gave me a ride
toward the sun just rising over our
town, telling me with each shift how I
was going to get it, but I didn't care
because you would be there when I got home.

Hands

for Phil Brady

When he died she felt
beneath the sheet for his
hands, which once were orange
on her back in the jukebox glow,
now failed and beautiful
as Dürer's, cooling
to blue,
and then the nurse wept too.

She wanted to remember them,
the feel of them in her own,
the way they try to remember
themselves, hands, by carving bark,
hollowing clay,
memorizing on the cave wall,
tapping, fingering the stops
and the valves that follow the pen,
or painting with, plucking and weaving,
the hair of the dead.

They begin tracing
their shape on paper, pressing
signatures in sand.
They end scribbling
like crabs,
reading the braille
of faces,
trembling,
feeding quarters
to the wrong dream.

Athletes Dying Young

If I walked onto a field today they'd call me Pops, and I couldn't bend over for a grounder or a suede glove. I might be better now, though, with grass more like carpet, instead of the gophered corn rows I ran through more on ankles than feet, my shoes heavy and soaked in sweat from the day before, not these foam shoes today that seem made of mushroom. For football my skinny body was padded into Marilyn Monroe, thick corsets under pants of mothballed canvas. The pads now are light and foamy, yellow as fat under the skin, glazed with stretch nylon, sexy and squamous as snakeskin, showing your ass, and I had a good one before men had asses. I might even could lift these aluminum bats, hollow for weak wrists, these gloves like hands of bananas that almost close on the ball by themselves, with another glove inside like a condom to keep dust fine as ashes from under the nails of those too squeamish to cup and pour and rub it into the bat's grip thin as a shinbone. That inner glove might've stopped the frying of my palm by hardball clowns, bruising my chuff-meat to the bone. I tried to catch flies on a glove hard and flat as a dinner plate, one my father gave me, hoping I'd be the player he wanted to be. I still have it, lying somewhere like a bear paw. I bought my own later, oiled the pocket hollow as a saddle, and then when we played catch in the driveway, he got the old one, the kind he craved when he was a kid, state-of-the-art: pale as chicken skin, bruised in the center, with no laces to hold the fingers together, as good as any glove would ever get.

Tough

Get tough, you always said when I cried.
When you sent me to school for three days
with a broken arm, when I was sick,
tough.
I thought of you all those laps
of boot camp, three miles to the chow hall.
Maybe you got me through.

Well, I've done it now,
too much chow,
have a shadow-jogger I can't outrun, though
You can't let it get you down, and
It's a great life if you don't weaken,
dosing me with fish oil each morning,
rubbing me with camphor at night,
painting my tonsils. Keep moving, keep
going to school, church, tough
as your father made you.
I won every attendance award.

You said I never cried when I got a shot,
even as a baby. I'd just look at you
and stop. Now you're tied down
in a ward, to stop your wandering,
and naturally I jog, fighting it off.
Something's got me good,
and you too, both
of us going down
to gristle,
tough as they get.

All Hallows

These Halloweens today are anemic things,
done before dark, supervised and safe.
I can see through the window from my bath
how a mother guides her two,
blue alligator and small pumpkin—
enough to break your heart, to make you
not have kids, so clean and pure, before,
as my mother used to say, they step
in shit like the rest of us. Already,
they stall sullenly on the porch,
holding out for more.
Later the mother will inspect the loot
for poison and pins.
And it's snowing to boot.

I remember the real ones, didn't even start
till leaved, warm-winded night,
Mr. Lumpkin out in his sheet behind the shrubs
to make my sister pee in her tutu,
dodging cars in our dark suits,
the window I broke at the Ledbetter's,
their son blackmailing me for a month.
Those evenings lasted longer than the candy.
My mother not answering the door
after she ran out of even apples,
though the kids kept pounding and shouting—
the pumpkin in the window was on fire.
And now, white-gowned, she wanders through
the nursing home, with no idea of who she is,
and my father is a skeleton.

Soon, they won't even need to dress—
door to door they'll go as greenhouse mutants.
Now it's a trial run, getting used to masks.

Who remembers anymore
anyway what it all means?
Unless to celebrate
the warped and twisted things we'll be.

Bible Camp

I was too frail for Boy Scouts, she said,
but Bible Camp was different. Hadn't Jesus
been in the wilderness? Hadn't our ancestor
Sidney Lanier written "The Marshes of Glynn,"
where *As the marsh hen secretly builds*
on the watery sod / Behold I will build my nest
on the greatness of God? And every dawn under
the Spanish moss of my own water oak, the sky
bleeding, wouldn't I have to read my father's
Bible, with the zipper
and the tissue-thin gilt-edged leaves?

But horseflies stung me by the pool, and huge
green and purple bugs flew through the night to bang
on the screen that was half the cabin, crawled in
my bed, in the rotten egg showers.
On small islands in brackish lagoons,
wild pigs ran through our tents,
and the counselor, who heard me, homesick,
crying in the dark overhead, called me bad
sport, told how he'd swung out on the rope
above a creek and fell spread-eagled, landing
on the stump, his crotch spurting,
nearly bleeding to death.

And then it rained, and when I found it under
sandy leaves, the zipper half rusted shut,
the red words of Christ bleeding,
I cried harder.

Only Danny Clark and I didn't get Honor
Camper. *My son and Danny Clark*, my mother said.
So I never told her of the day we went
out to Jekyll Island on the yellow bus, the white

road of crushed shells a gauntlet between long
rows of palmetto and Spanish bayonet,
and we ran over the snake, a big diamondback.
I stood aside, afraid, as they
finished it off with sticks, tied it
across the fender. Somewhere
on the beach I lost my best
shirt, covered in cowboys and balloons,
looked all day, even in the pavilion
where teenagers danced and the jukebox
gave me, salty, wet, a buzz, where
the guide took the sand dollar I'd found
and said, *Here, I'll show you*
a miracle, and broke it open to get the cross
inside, then handed back the pieces.

I slept in the dunes, close as I could
to the fire, back too late from searching
to get a hot dog or blanket, crying this time
all night, shivering with cold and sand fleas.
I had stopped by the time light
came over the dunes, and I got up,
walked past the sleepers,
past the dead, smoking fire,
to where it lay, now gilded with sun,
and reached out and touched it,
ran my hand along the scales
that were dry as pages.

First Love

When they found out we wanted to get married
they stopped us from seeing each other,
and we had to sneak around until
I left for college. I finally cut
my wrists and sent a dozen roses,
writing *goodbye* on the card with my
bandaged hand. She went and married
somebody else. That family was too
close anyway, calling I love you
through the walls at night.
I didn't know about Freud then.

The last time mother saw her she had
two kids and weighed in around two
hundred, which is two hundred too few.
I wonder if her husband rides
a motorcycle like her father did.
He wouldn't understand poetry,
how you can't hit a pothole with it,
or slide a hundred yards on gravel,
showing the scars of leather
to your son-in-law. He's probably
dead by now, and I liked him.

After twenty years, this started out as my
revenge, but turned into a typical
poem: a motorcycle, two kids, some
scars, and a fat wife calling
I love you through the walls at night.

Tying a Tie

I saw you naked
only once, walking from the bedroom
to the bath. I'd never seen hair
that black. When you came back
you held a towel there.
Once I watched while you put on
one of those starched white shirts,
tucking the tails between your legs.
But I needed to know the right
way to shower, wash my hair, shave.
Or how to tie a tie,
a Windsor knot or that other one.
Maybe you didn't know.
I still don't know
if I do things right,
if everybody reaches through their fly
and pulls their underpants down to pee.

Much less sex. So when I got
into trouble, you said, *You've*
destroyed everything we ever tried to build
up in this community.
And God forbid I ever miss church four times
a week, even once a year to watch
The Wizard of Oz on Sunday night.
I still dream about those no's,
wake up crying, pounding on your chest
even in your coffin. You don't seem to
mind, or even notice.
God comes first, you said.

Well, God has you now, maybe teaching you
about that loop on the back
of the big end that the little end goes through.

The Date

Even she would get them mixed up.
After he died, in the Social Security office
she turned red, stuttering my sister's
birthdays, their marriage dates, her
ages, his. Don't tell her, she said
outside, she'll think she wasn't
wanted. Conceived on a furlough
at *her* sister's house,
but when?

So how can I know when
she went riding her bike
up to Lakewood Heights, to Schwartz's
drugstore to sit giggling with her friend,
giving hell to the skinny preacher's
son in glasses and apron who wiped
the table, too stuck
up to speak, so much
older, robbing the cradle, robbing
the Fulton High basketball team,
her drunken butcher father, her flapper
mother. Or when they met there
outside after work the first
time, or when they eloped to some
justice of the peace in the middle
of some night?

Now nobody can even remember when
he died, exactly. And it didn't have a name,
exactly, just a phone booth by the road.
And she's in a home and can't
remember anything
at all.
All we know

is they were born—1925, she said one
time, 1920 another—at the Heights,
whether they were wanted or not.

The Time

The time the ladder cracked like a bad tooth
and I began to fall two stories
from where I hammered nails into the dark
ceiling like the inside of a helmet.
The time the rung snapped like a shin
when they said it wouldn't.
Oh, I'd been up aluminum ladders, loaded,
bouncing like a rope bridge toward the top
with my 60-pound pack of shingles already oozing
tar in the August Georgia sun: the bouncing
gave; you were afraid, fine. But wood was firm.

The time the half-track hit a hole
and my father's seat cushion slipped,
his spine giving to the iron rail,
the months, no, year in a body cast,
the troop ship pulling out with all his pals.

The time I finally got into a game,
recovered a fumble I couldn't help falling on,
and they carried me on their shoulders down
my street, then suddenly threw me off,
my legs splayed over my head, to land
on my butt-bone on the asphalt
and lie quietly trying to remember what breath was
and where I'd had it last, so much I'd lost it seemed
to be puffing a dot of sail over the horizon,
even the baby's spoonful I needed back to speak.
The time they carried me home white as the sheet
I'd lie under for weeks.

The time the ladder broke, and I
twisted like a cat, and gave at the last like
a paratrooper in a bad country to be crippled,

squatted on the concrete, soles stinging,
waiting for cracks to begin and spread.
The time his outfit had 90 percent
casualties at the Battle of the Bulge.
The time I stood and walked away.

The Song of Calling Rain to Rain

Because so many of our parts
have spares—breast, arm, eye—we must
need pairs, so much
of the universe about
attraction and loss—stones
parted by glaciers or continents
colliding like ships, rivers
prised apart in agitation
and leaping in reunion, tired
tree leaning on tree, no
wonder things huddle when they can—
rubble, leaves, grapes, more leaves, waves.

As my mother approaches mere
matter again, she wanders all night like a moon
seeking mother, husband, friends
from grammar school, pats
puppies long dead. Sometimes I can
forget she's locked in a room
down South, as she has forgotten our names.

The Shona pull rocks from the earth
and carve out what's inside,
believe all things want release
as smoke wants out of wood and back
into the sky, say when shelves of rock
ring in the rain, it's a song of reunion,
which is a song of separation.

We hope she will go ahead
and die. In her room is a phone
with numbers she can't read,
though she's never forgotten a face.

Gray

It's there all along, waiting
like ink in a well or sky before dawn,
but it isn't easy to die.
You have to betray the body, cut loose
the two fish gasping at the end
of invisible line, the heart
trying to twist free, the brain
sucking straws for the last blood.

We walk through gray stones to choose
hers, and our own, through live oak shade,
following the middle names, a strand
in braided lives, a Babel rope up
a tower where no princess lives.
This is a model of the haunted world,
a city where meanings genuflect behind
intentions. But the snotty dead won't talk to us;
they've moved uphill, graduated, left the home
of their little brothers and sisters,
wet behind the ears. Ears themselves must seem
contemptible to them now, like training wheels.
What dog whistles they can hear! And how
insufferable that they can't suffer,
that they have this big secret.
But it's a club, their treehouse ladder nailed
right through the bark, right into the sweet meat until
sap oozes the nail holes.

We gave her morphine till the end,
watched the hair float upward like ash,
gave the morticians a picture
to set it right again, fluffy as mimosa,
that color of sky right after black.

II *The Place Names of Dreams*

Small Road to Nowhere

I live on a hill with troubles,
mine, every one of them, everywhere
like the struck-back teeth of cemeteries.
The last one I had to haul up
myself, and it almost killed me.
But now it sits quiet in the back room,
dusty, tied like a ham and still
as the swing in the front yard
where gnats swarm and orbit an atom.
I only go to town for feed
and seed, and haircuts where the pole
spools its red, white, and blue ribbons
endlessly. Two chairs, no waiting.

Driving Toward the Ocean in the Afternoon

Every place is real
when you stop. A flat,
and there you are
where a blade of grass
lives with its spider, a stone resting
where it has since the road was built
over where it lay a long time before that.
This bush has always grown
in exhaust and burst of car wind.

The silence comes welling up
like clear water through sand,
clouds look on from their
blue distance, above shrimp
and shad swarming along
the surface, sawtooth trout
their shadow, their reflection,
gull flocks.

You begin to change the tire,
pushing that stone
a little closer.

Bayou

I don't go to the Gulf anymore
to wade out before dawn from shore
into water warmer than the air,
gulls and dolphins everywhere,
and, feeling with my feet the washboard sand,
shuffle to the edge of where I stand
and, having gone as far as I can go,
cast my line toward Mexico.

I live now where color gives in to snow,
but I feel in my blood how they know
in the fall to enter the marshes, out
of the roughening sea, the trout
moving in on an autumn tide
to feed on the shrimp and crabs that hide
in the prairie edge of green sawgrass,
the sky finally blue with the first pass
of northern air so strong
reeds bend that were straight all summer long.

These tidal rivers become in dreams
skewed kinds of northern streams—
theater or supermarket aisle,
a furniture showroom with pile
carpet rippled like sand
under water now clear, where I stand
on sofa, or island of cans, and cast
to where I saw their fin-flick last.
And when nothing I own will make them bite,
I jump from bed to bed in fluorescent light,
from room to room, following behind
their search for the sea they'll never find.
And finally, near dawn, snow falling outside,
the fish begin moving in my own tide,

ebbing in the dark aisles of me,
looking for an inland sea
where tides and weather
are quiet together,
and the dark water in the smallest bay
rises and falls on the heron's leg
barely an inch all day.

Every Reason

The airport shuttle almost hits
the car with *Just Married* in shoe
polish. *They had every reason to live,*
the papers always say, as if you needed
all of them, as planes need a
destination, power, *and* beauty to stay up.
Their sleek bodies of light blur in earth's
heat like the shimmer of water.

November and warm, from above, the trees' long
shadows over the clearings like lashes,
the barns white as toothpaste.
We still have the landing, then the two-lane road, four
lanes to drunks. Why did we ever leave?
What were we looking for? And I just got
a new job. But there's always a reason—if
not a baby, then the pregnancy, or the falling
in love, and on back to the first departure and
arrival. The fields are spongy green amid the sepia,
the mattress batting of stripped trees. The sky
is extra blue, and the clouds so new
you can still see the brush strokes. O God,
if we ever get home, we'll never leave again.
Or if we do, we won't stay.

Between Pittsburgh and Cleveland

What you notice first when you move
here is houses boarded like bandaged heads,
the ice-bound ships of empty steel mills,
old people sliding,
rusted cars spinning,
through slush
that packs and blackens behind wheels,
drops and lies in the road
like dead stars.

Next Sunday the Steelers play the Browns
but no one will watch—
we don't give one hundred and ten percent,
we don't take one game at a time.
We put on our pants one leg at a time,
and we sit on the bed to do it.
We're not going to rally
or regain the momentum.

Our sport is getting through the day,
the way in Scotland they run in only
jogging shoes up "fells," then back down
on paths of stones like bowling balls.

They say, we know this hill
can break bones.
We want to see if it will.

Advent

Kids have sprayed the boulder
orange, given it
black eyes, a stitched
mouth. My neighbor tells
about the ferry, how
birds at the edges of great
bodies of water, whirling
in the white skies like pepper,
wait for blue weather, play
statues with a winter
that can open one gray eye
and freeze them halfway
across. We hang out suet,
sow millet, as if winter
were another crop, snow warm
as cotton, sleet nourishing
as rice we would die without.
The leggy marigolds we pulled up
lie on the driveway
still pushing out their suns,
and we begin piling leaves,
stuffing them in plastic
sacks, stacking
the pillows so high
it must seem to the circling
birds, to the squirrels in their
holes, to the knuckleheaded
jack-o'-lantern in the park,
that we are hoping someone
will fall and save us.

Rust Belt

After a year here we learn
they have a name, *Beaters—*
the ones without insurance
who don't give a shit,
who drive out-of-control
toboggans and just hope they slide
into one of those Jap cars with their huge
rusted Chevys, Fords, Pontiacs
with the big names, eaten so bad
they're just frames.
He gets welfare for cigarettes
and lotto, limps through the grocery
buying dented cans and no-name stuff,
leaves mufflers and tail pipes
in the road, curses me in my car
he didn't make, didn't pour
into a mold then piece together
because some hotshot thought small
cars were a fad, no fins.
He snorts at the poetry reading
in the paper—*Poems. That's what*
we're making now—
and after the reading, while
we're out looking at the Amish drive
their black sleighs, he keys a Subaru, slips
skating across the parking lot in old shoes,
and cheap wine drips from the bag
like a lung. If we were there we couldn't help
laughing, and he wouldn't even mind
because he knows people like us,
the ones who think they'll somehow get to the future
before he does.

Winter in the South

Somewhere a thousand miles down
there's a silence between tin-roofed farms,
corn stubble, and the steel wool
of distant trees I owned on days
the gray clouds swirled and combed
like hair, lighter where the sun
yellows as it sets.

It's not cold but has been,
the clay paths spewed up
in red ice, everything still
and vertical as nails, sepia
photograph of rain. A far-off pan
of lake, cleaned of brush by the cold,
is a puddle in a yard of brown grass.

I follow trails across clearings of that
knee-high hay-grass no one knows the name of,
the arms of every oak at the woods'
edge holding shadow
like an X ray, every pine
layering its darkness. I know inside
the rusted shavings of leaves,
smell of leafmeal, broken strings
of pine needles.

Maybe one duck, circling the lake
before dark.

Hardheads

for Matt

Out in the brown tidal river, the snow of herons
and gulls covered mangrove islands. The sun rose
from dawn to full morning, the bridge hotter, whiter,
so still and quiet you could almost hear
the tide rising to cover holes of fiddler crabs
in black mud. Nothing but hardheads, with the slimy spine
that could puncture rubber soles, and one ray
whipping its tail, belly a white face
working, gills sad, down-turned clown eyes.

My grandfather, if it wasn't an Ex-Lax morning,
with his rusted reel and dry-rotted line;
my huge horny-handed plumber uncle
who'd untangle whiskery line all morning
out of the bottoms of his bifocals, smiling;
his son, blond brother to me; my father, fishing
for the aristocratic sea trout he never caught,
his captain's hat, his rod pulling the current
like a question mark. *There he is!* he'd shout
and whip his rod around, knocking off his hat.
That was a definite strike. Then back to waiting
as the sun moved toward afternoon.

All dead now. Plastic reels. A hook through shrimp
that wanted loose from shell. The plumb bob of sinker
to reach the bottom, catch another one,
my uncle laying down his rod, smiling, poking pliers
down the bony throat, throwing it back
to splash beneath the grid they raised
for the marlin-gaffed boats of fat men drinking beer,
headed for the blue. Sometimes a car would come by,
fanning us with hot air, tires bumping
on the tarry seams of the bridge
like heartbeats. And after, the silence
I haven't heard since.

Fortified Hills

I will lift up mine eyes unto the hills,
from whence cometh my help.
—Psalm 121

It looked like a courthouse
stranded when its country moved on,
white columned as any plantation,
black and white inside
as a Tudor house, another Baptist
auditorium, named for Sherman's
guns that overlooked and torched
Atlanta, no good lifting their eyes
to us. We thought preachers meant
our hills in particular, forty-
five of them, though we counted only
one. Parents sold it to The Niggers
rather than let even one inside,
stripped, moved it to the suburbs, built
another in a wound of red earth—new
columns, new auditorium.

In dreams it's empty, ancestral home, all
attic, all ghosts, every bulb-lit
basement room only I knew,
lawnmowers in slanted dark
under stairs, scarred cork
bulletin boards, hymnals
shredded to the bark, inch
of water in pebbled green vases,
balcony that creaked when no one
tiptoed around it, blood-red carpet
everyone I ever loved walked down
Just As They Were.

Or it's full of new families, no one
remembering, no place for me but in
the baptistry, Preacher Daniel

showing me again how to pray
holding my nose, smelling the rubber
of my white robe until I can't
breathe, strangers watching
as I go down into, then under
that warm Jordan whose light
wobbles on the painted wall of palms.

The Great Northern Possum

Everybody in Mississippi had one,
little fat, dim-witted things,
first in headlights on a hot night,
windows down, twangy music on the radio
about squashed hearts,
then by piney roads at sunrise,
the buzzards maybe half
an hour away.

The Possum Poem Club used to meet
in a bar called The Road Kill
on Sundays, and it was a big club.
We'd say,
To swerve might make more dead,
and hammer it home: drive
in a kind of yellow trance,
brake leg so heavy it won't lift.

But here? With snow and rust
everywhere,
in the middle of the day, sun
yellowing the clouds, lumbering
out like the southern type, never even
pausing when I swerved on ice,
pigheaded?

Wouldn't it have made a great
poem? Empty steel mills, crows
headed south, Vivaldi on the radio,
and blood on the snow?

The Original Adam and Eve

They've been found in Mesopotamia,
Ohio, in a sideshow, "unearthed"
says the canvas where he's painted
a pink David, she, Botticelli's Venus,
a python coiled between like a stack
of tires, tongue forking the air.
Inside they're enough
to demand your money back,
"serpent" segmented and thin
as a worm, bat's pointed ears and pig
nose, still tangled in her legs
like the cord of a child who is gone.
She's four feet tall, so hairy
her small breasts almost invisible,
grasping feet cupping air, sad
monkey face.
He's maybe an inch taller, fingers
crabbed with arthritis,
side squashed in where the rib was.
The fig leaves are faded gray as bay leaves
and brittle, broken to show their sex
shrunken, almost gone.
The government has stepped in,
and after a long tour they'll be buried
for good, two little hills with a ridge between.

The Place Names of Dreams

We walk dark streets where all
our houses are, the one we were
born in, where we live now.
The one we will die in is across the street.
They all have names, like in England,
scrollery burned in redwood: Seaview,
Driftwood, Winter, Rose Cottage, 1960, Florida,
Mother. Right over there is the sea, or
a lake, three cabins in the mountains, Scotland,
its lilac heather growing up the steps
into all the houses. Walking under
trees or streetlights, we pass everyone we've
known as they turn to go in, their
names on the doors and mailboxes, smiling over
their shoulders as they take in newspapers, flowers, pink
letters, gather in from the twilight
children we never knew they had, children we
were, or become as we follow them
past the fence into the woods we
got lost in, blowing the tin disc from
a doll's belly to scare away ghosts,
into the backyard, the garden where we lost
the harmonica we got for a birthday,
rusting somewhere in the darkening wet
grass after the summer sun goes down
and stars and honeysuckle come out, and we
have to go in for the last time, wading
through colored leaves, swimming in blue
wood smoke toward the house with no
windows and no name.

New House on the Market

Needs work but has character,
rosewood mahogany everywhere, blood
velvet runners and drapes, orange
light in sconces like a theater lobby
of the twenties. A pair of
slippers still on the radiator.
He was a philosopher, old
postcards of the Masters thumbtacked
to the cracked yellow walls, white
beneath like skin under a scab.
They counted over four thousand books
in one small room where a child had slept.
After the collectors finish, they'll be
given away, and when I get home I'll start
giving mine back to the used book and garage
sales, sending them on ahead like a pool
of raindrops back to the clouds, like souls,
winged and white between dark covers, back
to a table with a sign that says everything must go.

Moving

Upstairs is easy, nearer heaven.
It's the basement where the chickens
have come to roost without your knowing,
where the piper has been playing low
for years. Or,
said another way, for saying
is easier than packing,
the sediment of your life
has sifted down through all these floors
like the lees of a wine
just ready to drink
or turn sour.

This is the first layer of the dig,
where the natives all were young,
kept artifacts and fetishes, slept
on the ground beside the fire,
sang, played instruments of wind
and string, brewed primitive beers
and wines, wove and sewed, and painted
on the walls the things they'd do and did.

Now we sift the rubble
of these early people.
Who were they,
and why did they leave?
Everything still as they left it,
as if they were only
going away for a short time,
as if they were coming back.

At Worm's Head

A dragon lives forever
But not so little boys . . .
"Puff, the Magic Dragon"

And I am dumb to tell the lover's tomb
How at my sheet goes the same crooked worm.
—Dylan Thomas

The island the Vikings called dragon (*wurm*)
steams out into the Bristol Channel,
the shipwreck graveyard
of the white-cap, ice-cap sea.
Vast currents at cross-purposes
make tides and winds without dreams,
cold enough even this July to sting
your head empty of willow rivers or palm trees.
Beyond mythology, its nostril smoke
this evening is the campfire of some kid
like Dylan who stayed too late and got caught.
It's no Puff—it's name is Rock, child
of Rock, grandchild of Rock, and the stones
we've piled together to hide behind
and give names like Sea View, on storm nights
shake, want to break apart and rejoin
ancestors that use the winds to call
to them half-buried from heather.
But the sea wrack is always new, though it's been
through many evening births
and it wreathes and combs the trees that point
away from here to quiet places in the combes
of country sleep, where the homes have names
and can mean them, where the drowned don't moan
down the chimneys at night, and we don't dream
of dragons or worms.

The Goodwin Sands

The deep moans round with many voices.
—Alfred, Lord Tennyson

I could throw a bone from this shingle and hit
the ship swallower, quick sands where
snapstick schooners foundered while
gales boiled them like chicken carcasses,
picked its teeth with spars and masts,
bathed sailors back to babies, then
scoured them with craw grit, and even now
keeps driftwood models in a glass
belly called the Kellet Gut,
wrings and slaps sails
on a scrub board of frosted glass.

Everything washed up here
for pirates and smugglers gleaning
tides like gulls and pipers, their
cottages, smoky-beamed and plastered white,
a long body of black ribs, sand-packed.
On the map I buy, each ship's a silhouette,
already a darkness as it nears the black
hole whirlpool no prayers could
steer round, the throat no words
could go through, not
Dreadnought, Return, Reliance,
Victory, Success, nor *Providence, Penelope,*
Jesus, Mary, and Joseph.
I like best the ones who knew
going out: *Blind Fortune, Why*
Not, Marie Antoinette.
Not even the *Deutschland*'s nuns
and sailors caught just north
on the Kentish Knock, held up
like Christs in the rigging
while the waves iced them over.

Sometimes the sea gives up its dead,
nudged here to Dover Beach by squalls,
or dragged up sleeping in the hammock of the nets
that sift these shoals, snagging anchors, pulling
bones of men like birth from the bones of ships,
through the tackle, bellbuoys,
hawsers, whelked and bolted timbers of a thousand
seafood restaurants. They trawl for sole,
fish down so long both eyes are on the top.

Disserth

When one of us dies, this ginger jar will
hurt a long time, on the mantle like an urn.
Then the other too will die, still
childless, and they'll give away or burn

what's left. But this will go
to garage, fire, and antique sales,
where couples who hold and bump and buy won't know
inside's a day in Wales,

grandfather's village where we stopped to buy
a sweater, sausage rolls, toy sheep—
the sun breaking through the mist, a sky
to die for—and something that would keep

us both alive, inside, of local clay
fired hard and painted gray
with a twist of blue Teifi salmon head to tail
going around like a carousel.

The Lake of the Sky

After Labor Day, and everyone's gone
until the snows come, the motorboats
covered with canvas, and the other cabins
empty, though the sun's still hot,
unfiltered. I sit in the borrowed
hot tub under redwoods and read
this abandoned book on the Donner party,
which stopped just ten miles north of here,
exhausted, out of food in only October.

I fall in love with Tamsen
Donner, married to the leader, the
richest, because she's "slight and wiry," reminding
me of a woman I knew once, so that I dream
about her for the first time in years. She comes
dripping to the door of the big house
to hear me say *I've missed you so much.*
With her back to him she whispers, *I love you,*
but won't leave because of the kids.
Because I don't know where she is, I wake up
miserable, and because I can't find her I drive up
to the pass, where they boiled rawhide into glue
soup, lived in cabins and tents like
sewers, ate their dogs first.
Later a woman turned and saw her husband
's heart sizzling on a stick.

If God had done one of a hundred things, they'd all
have made it. Stopped even one storm that worst
winter ever. After struggling to catch up
for six months, they missed crossing the mountains
by only hours before the passes filled.
Stumps where they stood on the snow
to cut wood are high as two basketball hoops.

Forty-two dead, mostly men.
The women and children did best.

Tamsen sent her children on, wouldn't leave
her husband who'd slashed his hand
with a chisel. When soldiers got through
in the spring, only crazy Keseberg was left,
kept alive by eating her brain.
The soldier looked around at bones and hair and said,
Burn it, burn it all.

There were a thousand ironies—
like names: Hastings was the man who knew
a shortcut, then abandoned them.
Reed, called a murderer, was safe
in Sacramento but crawled back across
the mountains to try and save the rest.
Eddy's wife died while he carried
children over the mountains,
then came back too.
But Foster shot Indians for food.

Keseberg lived to start a restaurant,
till kids began to throw stones.

On the 13th green I reach out as if for
her, touch a pine and think,
this is my life, right
now, and I'll never have another.
On a path halfway around Fallen Leaf
Lake I sit on the stones of a ruined
cabin, eat a sandwich and think of Virginia
Reed, who finally made it out, writing back home,
We have left everything

but I don't care for that
we have got throw with our lives
but don't let this letter dishearten
anybody
never take no cutofs
and hurry along as fast as you can.

Magi

And a damn hard time we had.
Oh, it was kind of nice
at first, winter being
so bare and tidy,
the trailer parks glittering
like tinsel,
every bony tree holding a nest
of ivy or mistletoe,
the leaves settled into pile
carpet, the grass even greener, parklike around
and through the grays and browns,
every little shack or ranch-style strung
with bulbs that looked in daylight
like vines of withered fruit,
tacky little trees in the window
waiting for Nintendo or Barbie,
pickups in the rutted yards, whiskey under
the seat, gun-rack in the back,
brick churches, white crosses, fireworks
cheap.
Was it worth coming all the hell
the way here, the motels,
the fast food, the rest stop graffiti?
And in the mountains snow like a
mother, the semis spraying salt
and slush?
Anything would have been.

Nineveh

We take turns consoling one another
about the lacks—subways, flowers, barbeque.
Tell how each came here, the try to get away
en route, the stinking, slimy water, a scum
of suds and fish bones floating, the ribbed dark.
This is better than that
some days. The steel stacks have stopped
smoking, empty guns.
Why was it so important
we be here
and not somewhere else?
At this time
and not another?

The snow starts again, scattering, each flake lost
and lonely in its halo of air
like the space around each star,
or that second before the end
of the chain when the running dog believes
this time he might make it.

III *How the Dead Bury the Dead*

Seventh Heaven

The first is just long, years and years to see how "more time" was just an excuse. You still don't learn to play the violin. You blame your parents.

This takes a while, a lot of umbrage taking, yelling, like a long Thanksgiving dinner. You blame yours, they blame theirs, you all cry, apologize, that sort of thing.

The third is sex, getting it out of the way, fifty years tops to work through combinations, permutations. By the end, you're sick of skin, and irritable. If only you'd gotten the chance the first time.

Bosses, cheerleader and Nobel committees, coaches and pro scouts, all the way back to Miss Marcus in the second grade, now they're impressed. You were the greatest thing since angel food. They apologize.

You need a rest. For the first two thousand, you do, you rest, but you hit the wall at four, think you're going to crack, so much solitude. It's as if you're a mountaintop, snow and clouds, all glare and wind. But you don't crack, or if you do it's more the snapping of a flag.

It's just more loneliness at first, six is, sort of like those first days of all your deaths, disoriented, cold. You're squeaking like something in the wind, splashing like a shore. There are thoughts, feelings, and memories but they're loosening leaves. There's the smell of smoke and lots of sky. You almost feel like letting go, falling.

You do.

Prayers

What keeps them from being like
letters—how you know sometimes when they're
        received, but you never know
when they aren't? Like bad luck, disease, or
        dismemberment, the limb
insurance companies always want to buy,
you know when it happens, but when it doesn't,
what have you been paying for?
        Or bear bells. Once on one of those
nature films with interpretive music a
        grizzly, down through the long tunnel of
        telephoto, smells hikers coming
and scrams. But when they come around the bend
        dressed in their smell, jingling their
        steps, all the hikers see
is an autumn path without the Haydn. Had one
been thinking the whole trip *Please, God,*
        no bears and did it work?
And who took those pictures, and would they have kept
  filming
if the bear hadn't run, or could they have pulled
        a rifle? Who would've had the sense to pray
        Or if there are bears, Lord,
let somebody be watching with nothing
        less than a 30.06, with the cross
        hairs of a telescopic sight?
Where is the soundtrack of *our* lives?
Where do those prayers go, those
letters? In a chest in an attic in the sky?
Over in the corner, stacked like a cord of wood,
the phantom limbs we never used?

Archeology

You're born with a bag on your back.
For a while you don't notice it,
or if you do, you sort of like it,
the way it flutters behind when you run
like Superman's cape. One day you notice it's
getting heavy, as if someone's put in
a stone for every year. You can't jump
as high, your shoulders start to bow, your knees
bend, it's harder to get out of bed after crushing the one you've
been lying
on. You strengthen the knees, stand straighter, shoulders
back, lie on the bottom, consider getting something
taken off or out. Just when you start getting
smug, you look down. Your feet are sinking
into the ground! Then your ankles, then
your knees. How do you walk with a bag
of rocks on your back, pulling your
shins from the earth?

Finally but slowly,
you can barely move at all, and
when you can't hold your nose
out any longer, you go under.
Rain washes, wind blows
away dirt, flesh, the rotten bag.
Someone comes by. They look at the pile
of stones and bones and say,
Something happened here.

Skin

Something's under it like moles,
prickling like cold wind rippling a lake,
sucking the way a magnet thrums the telephone's
membrane burring out its bad news.
Skin is your friend:
imagine a big frog leg, flayed,
wind and sand on bare muscles, rain
in grooves sluicing bones, and you
know why slick organ bags
glue skin like wet paper.

It's the first to go—in earth,
peppering like buckshot, in fire,
shrinking and crackling.
Because it never bleeds it's
the part lovers love, smooth to the
tongue and sweet-smelling,
covering stuff like chicken gizzards
in blond gristle, the package we don't
want to open. Its mouths like
curtains open to let us in so far,
where a backdrop hides the gears and pulleys.
It's not the actor we want anyway,
but the character, in pancake and greasepaint.
It's the story we want, the shallow,
happy ending, not the asides, the
parenthesis that says beauty's
only skin deep, because that's
deep enough.

How the Dead Bury the Dead

This should have been the question
to Jesus, not *why*, all that philosophy,
but *how*, a little scientific curiosity.
Maybe it became a disciple joke. The answer?
With a pick and shovel? They'd giggle to themselves as they
straggled behind him. Or maybe the beginning of the knock-
knock joke, most biblical humor being
morbid, Martha saying of poor
Lazarus, *But, my Lord, by now he stinketh*, and breaking
everyone up.

But nobody asked, or wrote it down. What difference could it make
then, so near eternal life? But in those Dead Sea caves
was neither handbook nor *The Disciples' Big Book O' Jokes*,
which is a tragedy. Think about the savings!
Or the quiet, kissless wakes because
no one has lips. Or tears. Or casket wood to choose.
And what else have they got to do? Bone idle, the British
say. And that was the way he said it, *Let the dead bury
the dead*, as if they'd been waiting to, the real unemployed.

Perhaps it's a potion you pour, a dust sprinkled on the
graves that pulls them to the top
like Clearasil. Maybe just leaving the bodies at
the edges of graveyards at sundown,
or wrapped on the curbs like garbage bags
brings them like the tooth fairies they were as apprentices.
From our beds we'll hear the clacking and sliding of knuckles
on the handles like more bones, and in the morning they'll be gone
beneath another anthill, and we'll be about
our business, their lives vanishing behind us
like dreams. And aren't there more

important things to do? After all, where were they going
in such an all-fired hurry they couldn't even take
the time to stick somebody in the ground?

Oh. And the answer? Almost anywhere. And as quickly as possible.

Tool

It's never the right one, size
or place, like love, whose names,
just as violent as vice—vise
grip, screw, straight-slot screwdriver,
wrench, socket—try to hold
together what doesn't want
to fit. Violent as my preacher father
building the cross that would be
my racer, no drill (How
often would he use one, anyway?), just
swearing and hacking that
bolt hole into an axle not even
Samson could turn with just a
rope. Half my fiber was splinters of
telephone poles. But he did one thing
right, at least once, because everything's
a tool when you need it, and the best are
near to hand, adjustable,
like the vise of chin and chest
when you dress a pillow,
or that jackhandle that can raise a woman
and you with her.

Epistle to the Church at Smyrna (Georgia)

. . . years that bring the philosophic mind.
—William Wordsworth

The night Mother found naked women
under the bath mat, I was in bed when she called,
Quite a collection you've got here.
Indeed, scissored from *Dude, Knight,* and *Gent.*
It took a minute to realize, to remember hiding them
when Clark called to offer to trade
Playboys. And then I wanted to die, to sink
beneath the covers like dark waters.

She made me burn them, their
peachy skins wrinkling, getting old all at once.
Later I found two *Knights* in her lingerie drawer,
and a bra with the tips cut out, volcanoes.

Those days I was a storm, a surf
beating against deserted beaches,
a sailor wandering with a bird around his neck.
You've destroyed everything we tried
to build up in this community,
my Baptist preacher father said.
This was after Mother left towels
under my stained sheets.
I blushed when I pulled back the spread.

One spring every day for a month
I'd come home from school and put on
the same shorts and shirt, and run
to play by myself all afternoon in the backyard
a game I invented for the Olympics, a game
of constant motion without time-outs
or time periods, a hurricane of sweat
with no eye, no calm, a ball small enough
to palm, and crowd roars after every score.

Mother must have watched from the window
and wondered if there was something wrong
with me. Once when I was playing guitar, she said,
A real man would be out hunting girls.

My father's gone to be with God,
my mother's in a home, wouldn't know a man
or a son from a bedpost, couldn't read a letter
even if I wrote one, about how I married
rather than burn, then burned anyway,
but finally don't think about sex
for days at a time, becalmed, floating
beneath clear sky and warm, glassy water,
waiting for the trades.

The Magic Flute

I'd just always thought no sperm
of mine would have, not the strength
exactly, but the interest in going
upstream, especially through rubber and
acids. But you were sleeping all day
every day, where we'd come, just north
of Dover Beach, to live for a while
without worries. I thought it a new
strain of jet lag.

So we had to go to London, to the special
clinic because of the thing in your brain
like a thermometer bulb that could
burst if you had a child or surgery,
but you began bleeding at the interval
of a play. *Hapgood,* wasn't it? And we took
the black taxi to St. Bart's where
in the middle of the night nurses
who looked like Florence Nightingale
wheeled you away through ancient
corridors, and I had to leave
you there, then got lost in dark
labyrinths, courtyards, and alleys leading
to more locked gates. I thought we'd be
forever in that underworld. *The only way
out is through,* you said. I said, *Don't
look back.*

And we lived happily ever after.
And what I remember is going to the doctor
the first time to find out, walking
scared and alone through the narrow
cobbled streets, seeing laid
out on the fishmonger's slab

a skate
on its back, all white belly and gutted,
in time to point and make you look
at a single rose growing through the sidewalk
ahead
and miss it.

The Texas Chainsaw Revival

Not souls, but bodies, nail-holed and
hungry, dem bones as promised rise up
from trapdoors of the local Boot Hill,
the reservoir gives up its bikinied dead, ski-rope-
tangled, weed-choked, propeller-gashed, hooked
with rubber bass worms, and the saints go
lurching through the streets, past the
De Sade Marquee (*Night of the Living Dead Parts*
XII & XIII), out to the edge of town where pickups
surround a tent lit like a lampshade,
go scraping down the sawdust aisle Just As They
Are toward what they were, where
the preacher in the shiny suit waits
with the hand still holding its Colt,
the head in its Stetson, a boot full of foot.
And God, God has the heart that will
fit like a bullet in the chamber.

Tenderhooks

My students live in houses
on the second floor, are just passengers
on the card game of life,
and are sometimes left dangling in left field.
They've had their brains washed out
and don't see the umpire's new clothes.

And this innocence complicates even
their young love, is why they put
their women on pedastools,
and why they're always ready to mount
the rear end of a dear as well as the front,
or see the partner's misery in the other half
of a felationship, see towers and trees
as phalanx symbols, need two to tangle,
forget to include diaphragms
in their research papers, and thus
take love for granite.

But they also know, from the standpoint
of observation, that we have become so content
on making snap judgments
that we often make them in haste,
that sex is becoming more freely practiced
by the general public to satisfy
their sexual needs and desires,
and that almost half of all pregnancies
occur within six months of intercourse.
That William B. Yeast gave rise
to modern poetry. That Chaucer took the nut
of love, cracked it, and laid the meat on the table.
That it is necessary that society abandon
its prejudices, and behave respectably
under the pretense that homosexuals
are human beings.

They use their brains and not just their bronze.
They do not go Gentile into that good night.
And if they have to shoot, they only shoot
the fat. They know
the cloud with the silver lining
will pull through. They are a Godscent.

Intensive Care

Like father, like son. Here
where he died, they come
for blood at night, and I wear
a pouch that throws my pulse
in spikes on a screen in another
room, and would go off like a factory
whistle if I tried to quit.
On other walls I've seen my radium
blood turn lungs to coal logs,
show my brain a firefly swarm.
Once they held a microphone to my heart
like an interview of an athlete,
but on the monitor behind I saw
something phosphorescent
swimming through the dark like a jellyfish.

It's like staying home from school,
all those ears at my breast, going like the bumper
cars that made me run
crying to Mama once. The heart has numbers
down a long row, nurses catch and measure
everything going in or coming out of me,
cover my chest with nipples, or limpet mines.
I sprout like the spider plant in my window.
Last night I dreamed it was the end
of the world, people running and screaming,
tea kettles left on stoves and going off.
This morning the nurse woke me for more
blood from another print walking the steep
vein up my arm. Only her white
glowed in the dark—*Hot*
time last night, she said,
had two of them go bad.

Today they'll take and roll
me on a spit to slice

shives of brain so thin
they'll hold them up and see
through to light, then bring me back
to this room to wait.
That's why they call us patients.
Straight ahead is a clock with second
hand, a calendar that says
To-Day is the thirteenth.
I like the hyphen, the *o*
an Ω, but modern like
the Christ on the wall by the clock—
on the cross, but not nailed down,
his arms out like a horseshoe.

The History of Effects

The Bible was created by Bishop Ussher
in 4004 B.C. Then Galileo cooked the universe
too long, and the earth, like a yolk, slipped off
center and everything began to wobble.
Freud needed a reason to talk about sex,
and Marx wrote a bestseller
so he could retire rich.
When the species started to hunt
for their origin, they discovered Darwin.

So now the ears of corn put down
tethers to the earth, trees rake
the wind into piles, the sun turns the world
like a ballerina, the way a magnet whirls
a rotor. Silence squelches the radios,
and darkness the bulbs. Automobiles are invented
to reach the malls, and choppers to haul
body bags, and animals come to live with us
to quench our loneliness and nourish our hunger.
We've begun to love the people who need us
as dandruff rises from sweaters to infect our hair,
and parachutes are the white flags
of suicides that fail.

The Gospel of Peter

Because I kept putting it off (let
this cup pass from me), it's Good Friday
when I have my surgery. Nothing serious,
just slicing, then reaming the roots
with bristles like a pipe cleaner.
Stitches. Major drugs. A gas mask
like a pig's nose. My wife has to wait
and drive me home. I'm worthless
the rest of the day, holding ice
against my face that falls
when I sleep. I watch a movie,
Spartacus, a crucifixion,
read Chekhov's "The Student,"
another crucifixion. It's coincidence
or conspiracy. A friend's in the hospital
losing her womb.

I feel sorry for myself, try eating to cheer
up, mumbling little zeroes in tomato sauce.
At the party they're having wine and finger foods,
the kind of stuff that got me into this mess—
the inside of my mouth
as though I'd eaten glass,
or the beaks and claws
of all the words I ever said
but didn't mean.

Job

When I lost my job, I wanted to go
out and get drunk. But the doc
took me off the booze, said my liver
had too much iron, was "stockpiling,"
like a war. When he told me my liver
was bad, I wanted to go out
and get drunk.

Friends say ignore him,
but my grandfather died of liver,
my father died of heart,
and my mother doesn't remember either
one, or me.

So much cancer around,
sometimes I feel like I'm walking through
a cauliflower farm.

My wife's at the male. I mean *mall.*

When he said, *You can drink*
or you can die, I said, *I'm*
thinking, I'm thinking, like Jack
Benny when the robber says your money
or your life,
or the drowning guy
no one would save because
he was a professor with a lisp.

The doctor frowned: just doing his job.

And my career? I get postcards:
If you're thinking of applying,
don't.

My children
have never even been
born, and they're sharper than a serpent's tooth
about it, sharper than piles, or these boils.

Did I mention the doctor took me off
liquor?
And that my wife's at the male
buying iron?

I fish most days.
I want the big one,
big enough to swallow a man.
I'd like to see that
professor, puked up,
walking away,
smarter than ever.

November Whiskey

So I wouldn't go to Nam after all.
I'd be like a mahout, who takes his
elephant down to scrub in the river each day.
Mine was the F-8 Crusader, with a gator,
not a knight, dancing by the big NW on the tail,
and like an elephant—big, gray, graceful—
could kill you, crush or suck you up,
but let me crawl it like an ant,
feed it with a fire hose, pump its veins
taut with red hydraulic fluid,
pull out nerves and black organs, lay them flat,
then put them back, bolt
pods to its stitched flanks.
Let me sit like a brain in its clear head,
in the middle of swamp, in the near-equatorial
sun and say November Whiskey
to the tower that could almost see across
the river to where strippers danced on Bourbon Street bars,
or talk to Foxtrot Tango, a giant erne that hunted
sub shadows in the blue Gulf.
Sometimes the wings were swans',
folded over its back,
sometimes stiff as a great white's fins,
and I'd sleep off hangovers in the gasping
mouth under the sharp nose, knowing
if it woke I'd be sucked down, not
like Jonah but Ahab into that vortex, that shredder.
With koala ears on, and dodging the big
slingshot, the draft that could fluke me
overboard, I'd launch it from runway or
whale-back carrier, the pilot a black bee eye,
the roar everywhere like a bubble my signals
danced in, a dragon I could lead with one hand,
its fire for someone else.

Heart Shot

A teacher was shot today, not
the regular, home with a cold. *His*
last thought would have been
revenge, but the one who got it only
had time enough to think, *do I*
know you? We know the kind who stayed
home, holding up unused
tickets for bulbs to pop at
when the plane goes down, his taxi late.
They miss it all the time, disaster,
these darlings of God—never even lose
car keys without missing by seconds ice
on curves, falling bricks, semis clapping
like dry hands. Everything's
significant, has a
reason—when the bullets start they're wearing
the dentist's lead bib, silver
cigarette case across the heart from some
beauty. They're Tokyo the day
they dropped it, gray, bitching how
it's just my luck, would rain
today, etc., while Hiroshima brimmed
with sunshine, lovers, and dogs.
Which brings us to the ones like
us, we never hear about, running
late, headed for the ice, the brick, the odd
bullet, lucking out, getting the last
seats, the sunny day—substitutes—
thick glasses, yellow tie, mouths
to feed, in front of
blackboards dodging
airplanes and spitballs, guys
named Henry who can use the work.

No Swimming

They're pulling someone out of the water
who shouldn't have been in it.
Here by this northern sea I remember
my deaths by water, the first, riding
smugly the floodwaters, canoe slipping
from under me like a hammock, cushions just
out of reach, my boots buckets
then anvils. I shivered and waved
from that sandbar a long time.

And then riding my girl on my shoulders
in the lake, her welted latex crotch
around my neck, the smell, until I stepped
off into deep water and she rode me down
holding my head like a pommel.
I sat on the bottom, crab
scrabbling till they pulled her off
and me back into the air I'd always loved
without knowing it.

The last time, I tried to cross
between the snaggle-toothed pilings of an old pier
to get to the other side where the surf was greener.
When I fell into a gum hole, my landing net
and stringer of sea trout wrapped me like a parcel
and the rinse cycle of the waves scrubbed me good
against the barnacles of the creosote logs.
I was going down for the third time
when something gave. Standing on shore again,
my knees shaking, bleeding, I held up in my left hand
the empty stringer, its cork that let the fish and me
escape, gone, my right hand cramped around the rod,
flapping at the end, a baby flounder.

Now they're kneeling, blowing into his mouth
as if he were a balloon, waving his arms
as if they could teach him to fly.

Apnea

Our souls sleep, and when we die, they come to life.
—Heraclitus

One is always suddenly
drowning,
one feels marbles
dropping
into her open mouth,
another's throat is stuffed
like a sausage with stringy pulp
of jack-o'-lantern.
The dreams turn bad for them—
the stillest water whirls,
the greenest yard floods into
swamp, boards warp and crack
over dark spaces.

For me there's merely a pause, a moment
between breezes when everyone stops
fighting, loving, showing me through my old
houses, and turns to me their faces of father-
wife-cousin,
to show alarm
at such stillness.
I've learned to stop,
to calm them all,
and for this anagram, this hiccup
of paean, the dictionary's sibilant
transient cessation of respiration
put down what I have,
and take my leave,
saying goodbye, saying don't
worry, it's not your fault,
what's wrong's outside the dream.
I must wake to breathe.

For My Friends, Who Complain That I Never Write Anything Happy

I should go with him in the gloom,
Hoping it might be so.
—Thomas Hardy

Once when I was building a church
out in the country, Christmas coming,
shingles glittering like tinsel, bare trees
still flocked with frost, we broke for lunch,
the other wood butchers and me,
and went looking, found a nothing little
roadhouse, and not expecting anything
since things smell better outside than in,
we sat and ordered the special—meatloaf,
sweet potatoes, turnip greens, and corn bread.
It was so good we almost couldn't climb
the ladder, sang carols like drunks all afternoon,
beating time with our hammers on nails.
I've never had anything like it before
or since.

Later the church burned down,
and I never could find that roadhouse again.
I've even lost the people who could prove
it happened at all, and though
it probably wouldn't be the same,
every Christmas I go home
and drive the back roads,
following no map
but my nose.

One Owner

It's got about a hundred thousand miles
on it, upholstery cracking, sometimes
a thumping
                              beneath the floorboard as if
something's coming through
                                        with a hammer.
The windows are yellowing,
                              and the wipers
can't keep ahead of the water. The tires
are balding, but who'd put new ones
on a heap like this?
                              Cockeyed headlights
split the difference of darkness.
                                        It smells too,
of old hair and sex, and now
there's a new sound,
     just loud enough
to be heard, definitely not
your imagination.
                              The needle is sinking.
There's a town up there somewhere
on the other side of static
with a station that plays nothing
but hits.
                              There it is again.
Can't you hear it? A sort
of gurgling.

Turn the radio up.
     Keep going.
                              The last exit was years ago.

Hypochondria

This week it's bladder
cancer for her, for me
Lou Gehrig's. You feel it
first in the wrists, like ice
water. But as Delmore Schwartz,
a famous sick man, once said,
even paranoids have enemies
and sometimes a cigar is just
exploding.
And someday it will come
for us, in some clothes or
other, some face, running
over the poppy fields like a perfume commercial.
Then we'll say we told you
so, and you'll feel a twinge
of guilt, and then another
in the back and just below
the shoulder blade, near the what,
the spleen?

Dying in the Fish Restaurant

Most people are happy to slip,
hit their head on a curb,
or clutch their heart in the subway.
No wonder the dead get so little
respect. I plan
a night of snow squalls, full
moon over the yellow sign—
Friday Night Special
Haddock $4.95.
I can see it all,
a spectator,
standing by the booth
I'm hogging, trying to chew
on the wrong side and still
taste, bitching at the waiter
how I like my slaw *with*
my fish, slicing down
the tip. When they find me in the men's room,
my fly's open, and my feet are sticking up,
a froth of snow around the soles
as if they'd been drinking beer.

Entrance

It's one of those days you wait for
all summer as if all your life.
Cool air has come blowing all day,
flickering tired green leaves.
You're so happy you could cry
and do, don't even care
if the drugstore's out of pills
because your brother's found work,
a building crew, wood butchers who
could use some part-time help,
like his smile and care less
if he never drives a nail.
So to the park, where,
remember, wind is springwater, quenching
the skin, blowing like a fall
you walk around in with the one
you loved most,
though everybody ever is there,
walking your way.
And the question is,
do you love them all, equally?
Sorry. Begin again.
It's one of those days you wait for
all summer as if all your life.

All of Us Are Children

floating down a river on our beds.
It's dark, and we're in pajamas,
though in the west, behind
the palms, there's a thread
of pink, a glow of violet,
as if we've just come in from play.
Each bed has a paper lantern
and we see each other in the glow.
Parents watch from verandas on the shore,
drinking together and hushing us,
but it does no good. When we're almost
quiet, giggling starts again
and spreads like wind over water.
Our beds are so close they nudge,
tip, and lap,
and goldfish rise to the light
through the reflections
of our faces.
Then the river opens
into a sea
we begin to fill
like a whole new sky,
and we are the stars.

ABOUT THE AUTHOR

William Greenway, a professor of English at Youngstown State University, has published two chapbooks and two full-length collections of poetry, *Pressure Under Grace* and *Where We've Been.* He holds a B.A. from Georgia State University and a Ph.D. from Tulane University. A native of Atlanta, William Greenway was named Georgia Author of the Year in 1994.

ABOUT THE BOOK

How the Dead Bury the Dead was designed and typeset in Quark XPress on a MacIntosh by Kachergis Book Design in Pittsboro, North Carolina. The typeface, Adobe Minion, was designed by Robert Slimbach and reflects the classical typography of the late Renaissance.

How the Dead Bury the Dead was printed on sixty-pound Glatfelter Opaque Recycled and bound by Thomson-Shore, Dexter, Michigan.